Master Sun's
Art of War

SUN TZU

孫子兵法

Master Sun's Art of War

Translated, with Introduction, by
Philip J. Ivanhoe

Hackett Publishing Company, Inc.
Indianapolis/Cambridge

15 14 13 12 11   1 2 3 4 5 6 7

For further information, please address
  Hackett Publishing Company, Inc.
  P.O. Box 44937
  Indianapolis, Indiana 46244-0937
  www.hackettpublishing.com

Photos by Galen R. Frysinger. All rights reserved.
Interior design and composition by Elizabeth L. Wilson
Printed at Sheridan Books, Inc.

Library of Congress Cataloging-in-Publication Data
Sunzi, 6th cent. B.C.
  [Sunzi bing fa. English]
  Master Sun's Art of war / Sun Tzu ; translated, with introduction, by Philip
J. Ivanhoe.
     p. cm.
  Includes bibliographical references and index.
  ISBN 978-1-60384-466-6 (pbk.) -- ISBN 978-1-60384-467-3 (cloth)
  I. Military art and science—Early works to 1800. I. Ivanhoe, P. J. II. Title.
  UI01.S93213 2011
  355.02—dc22   2010045535

The paper used in this publication meets the minimum requirements of
American National Standard for Information Sciences—Permanence of
Paper for Printed Library Materials, ANSI Z39.48–1984.

∞

For Admiral James Bond Stockdale,
Warrior, scholar, colleague, friend

永垂不朽

Contents

Acknowledgments

Those not wholly in the throes of delusion realize that while we are responsible for much that we do, we are not the sole authors of our own lives. Many other people and the subtle workings of fortune play too large a role to allow such a claim to stand. The same is true of scholarly works. These features of human life offer us more reasons to celebrate and enjoy our achievements. One of the great joys of having a hand in any scholarly work is to acknowledge those who have most directly contributed to bringing it forth. In this case, I want first to thank those with whom I served in the United States Marine Corps and Army and especially those who trained me. While at the time it was hard to see and impossible to appreciate, they taught me many lessons that have helped me not only in the present project but in almost every aspect of life. Within this group I wish to acknowledge a special and incalculable debt to the first Marine to train me: my father, John Joseph Ivanhoe. I also want to thank the various mentors who struggled to teach me Chinese and especially my first teachers, Professors Kao Kung-yi and Chuang Yin, who conveyed to me not only part of their vast knowledge and remarkable sense of the Chinese language but also their love and enthusiasm for Chinese culture. More immediately, I want to thank the colleagues and friends who offered corrections or comments on earlier drafts of this work: Erin M. Cline, Michael R. Slater, and Yu Kam-por. Special thanks to the Department of Public and Social Administration, City University of Hong Kong, for generously supporting this work and to Melanie J. Dorson and Justin Tiwald for carefully reading through and commenting on the entire manuscript. Finally and always, I want to thank the wonderful folks at Hackett Publishing Company, and especially Liz Wilson, for her splendid editing, and Deborah Wilkes, who have helped me in this and so many other endeavors.

Preface

This volume is offered as an introduction to the greatest Chinese military classic of all time: *Master Sun's Art of War*. I have endeavored to keep the volume focused on the text and toward that end have not included detailed accounts of its history and reception, the historical context in which it was written, recent archaeological finds that bear on the text, or the complex scholarly debates about its authorship. I have provided an introduction which touches on all these issues designed to enable the reader to approach the text with enough knowledge to appreciate its core ideas and general nature and which seeks to sketch some of the ways this remarkable work engages and throws light upon issues that range far beyond any field of battle or military conflict. For those interested in pursuing further the more technical issues regarding the text's history and composition, I have provided guidance in both notes and a list of recommended readings.

The cover depicts three of four horses from a team drawing a war chariot in the eight-thousand-man terracotta army of the First Emperor of the Qin Dynasty. Each of the chapter titles of the translation displays figures from this same collection. As readers can see, the face of each warrior in this massive array of figures is unique.

Introduction

War may not be *the* oldest profession, but surely it is among the oldest. It is also among the most unsettling and important: carrying dramatic, far-reaching, and often decisive consequences for both individuals and states. The significance of war is succinctly captured in the opening lines of *Master Sun's Art of War* (*Sunzi Bingfa* 孫子兵法):

> War is a major affair of state, the ground of life or death, the way of preservation or oblivion. One cannot fail to investigate and study it.

Even these brief observations should lead us to wonder why we do not find more systematic and penetrating reflections on the nature and conduct of war within the world's philosophical traditions. In the Western tradition, the two best-known examples of the genre are relatively late. Niccolò Machiavelli's *The Art of War* (*Dell'arte della guerra*) was published in 1521 and Carl von Clausewitz's *On War* (*Vom Kriege*) became available in 1832.[1] *Master Sun's Art of War* is far and away the oldest example of a sustained, philosophical reflection on the strategic, organizational, and political aspects of war. It is also the most important, having exerted immense influence not only on thousands of years of Chinese culture and the other cultures of East Asia, but more recently throughout the world. Its profound influence on Mao

---

1. Machiavelli's work is presented in dialogue form and reflects many ideas found in his more widely known and studied works on politics and states. Clausewitz's work was published posthumously; it existed as a manuscript when he died. His wife compiled and edited his work, leaving out later revisions. She completed the final two chapters either herself or with the assistance of an unidentified official. See Rupert Smith, *The Utility of Force: The Art of War in the Modern World* (London: Penguin Books, 2006), 57.

Zedong is well known;[2] through him and his writings, *Master Sun's Art of War* has inspired and guided many revolutionaries, as well as those who oppose them, throughout the twentieth century and into the twenty-first.[3] This remarkable longevity and enduring significance is only fitting for a work attributed to a man named "Sun the Martial" (Sun Wu 孫武)[4] and composed during what is known as the Warring States Period (Zhanguo shidai 戰國時代 403–221 BCE).

The extensive and increasingly broad influence of *Master Sun's Art of War* owes more to the nature of the text than to any aspect of its history. Had Sunzi focused on particular tactics or weaponry, his work would quickly have become dated and purely of historical interest.[5] His primary concern, though, was strategy, broadly construed, and it is this choice and his comprehensive approach to it that has made his work a perennial source not only for those interested in understanding and waging war but also for those who seek to apply his insights to other competitive endeavors, such as politics, business, or sport, where conflicts must be met and opponents overcome. Sunzi's particular perspective on war makes it especially versatile in application and extremely interesting politically. Unlike Mao Zedong, Sunzi argued explicitly and strongly against protracted military campaigns. As I shall argue below, this is because he saw war more as in tension with the political than as in any way an expression or extension of politics. War is a regular part of human experience and something one must prepare for and face

---

2. For Sunzi's influence on Mao's views on warfare, see Samuel B. Griffith, trans., *Sun Tzu: The Art of War*, Reprint (New York: Oxford University Press, 1971), 45–56.

3. The United States Marine Corps regards Mao's work "On Guerrilla Warfare," which took many ideas from *Master Sun's Art of War*, as important enough to warrant inclusion as a Fleet Marine Force Reference Publication. See http://www.scribd.com/doc/12891801/Marines-Mao-TseTung-on-Guerilla-Warfare.

4. Sun Wu is the surname (Sun) and personal name (Wu) of Sunzi ("Master Sun"). The honorific *zi* ("master") was commonly added to the surname of famous thinkers.

5. The only exception to this feature of the text is Chapter 12, which concerns using fire as a weapon. Even in this case, the treatment of the topic is broad enough to continue to have application.

squarely, but it is an aberration. For Sunzi, war is to peace as illness is to health. Illness is an inevitable part of life, but with the onset of illness the proper goal is to find a quick and decisive cure to return to health. Sunzi never glorifies war or revels even in the prospect of victory, and he is poignantly aware of how harmful war is to the welfare of states and the people within them. In these respects, *Master Sun's Art of War* is like the *Daodejing* and this is but one of several interesting similarities.

Master Sun's Art of War was composed in roughly the same period as the *Daodejing*, and both are composite texts whose final forms were greatly influenced by unknown editors. Both works are short, highly compact, and terse; *Master Sun's Art of War* is roughly six thousand characters in length, while the *Daodejing* is approximately five thousand characters long. *Master Sun's Art of War* and the *Daodejing* have proven remarkably influential throughout the course of Chinese history; both have profoundly influenced other East Asian cultures as well and in recent years have found a wide readership outside of East Asia, especially in the West. There are also significant differences between these two remarkable ancient classics. The *Daodejing* is a work of poetry; *Master Sun's Art of War* is a more analytical and systematic work written in prose. Sunzi's work has by far a clearer and more circumscribed topic: war. As a result, while both texts have been interpreted in diverse ways, the range of interpretive possibilities is narrower in the case of *Master Sun's Art of War*. The *Daodejing* has been understood as offering important lessons about warfare, economics, and business; modern interpreters have even managed to see in it lessons about physics and the philosophy of language. Nevertheless, it has most often been understood as concerned with ethical and spiritual matters and offering a vision of the proper way to live life and organize society. *Master Sun's Art of War* does not lend itself to such a wide range of readings; it does not offer lessons about ethics or spiritual matters, nor does it describe a way of life or ideal social order; it is a book about conflict and strategy; its sole purpose and aim is describing how to achieve victory.

The Text and Its Author

Master Sun's Art of War traditionally is thought to be the work of a single author, a man, as noted above, named "Sun the Martial," who lived and wrote in the late sixth to early fifth centuries BCE, thus making him a contemporary of Kongzi (Confucius). A strong consensus among modern scholars presents a very different view: The text is a composite from different sources, shaped by different hands, and dating from the early part of a much later era, the Warring States Period (403–221 BCE). The purported author is not a historical figure but an idealized personality; when the text records what "Master Sun" says, it is presenting material from a variety of different sources as the teachings of a single ancient military sage.[6] Nevertheless, too much can be made of these modern discoveries about the text and its author in at least two respects. First, we do not have a clear account of who put the text together or edited it into its present state, this may represent a long and varied process of accretion and editing or this process may have been quite limited in duration and the number of people involved. Second, the fact that a text is composed from a variety of disparate sources does not mean it lacks coherence or even a consistent style; an editor or editors can shape even extremely varied and inconsistent material into quite coherent and consistent wholes, just as a skilled quilter can produce a masterpiece by stitching together tattered and discarded pieces of cloth.

One of the most important advances in our understanding of the text and its authorship occurred as the result of a recent archaeological find. In 1972, a cluster of late–Han Dynasty tombs, dating from between 140 and 118 BCE, was unearthed at Mount Silver Sparrow (Yinque Shan 銀雀山) in modern Shandong. Among the artifacts

---

6. For the definitive study of this issue, see Jens Østergaard Petersen, "What's in a Name?: On the Sources Concerning Sun Wu," *Asia Major*, Third Series, 5, no. 1 (1992): 1–31. I will continue to refer to Sunzi as the author of the text but only as a kind of shorthand referring to those responsible for bringing the text to its present form.

discovered was a substantial cache of texts written on bamboo strips, among these were numerous military texts. Most of these texts were fragmented and incomplete, but they included the earliest known copy of *Master Sun's Art of War* and a previously unknown work called *Sun Bin's Art of War* (*Sun Bin Bingfa* 孫臏兵法). This latter work resolved a long-standing controversy about the figure Sun Bin. Traditionally, Sun Bin was regarded as a later descendant of Sunzi and the author of a "lost" work on the military arts. With the discoveries made at Mount Silver Sparrow and material more recently unearthed at other archaeological sites, we now can say with considerable confidence that Sunzi is a myth but Sun Bin is an actual historical person; a most remarkable man who lived, worked, and wrote in the fourth century BCE.[7]

Despite the fact that *Master Sun's Art of War* was not written by a single historical figure, the text quickly assumed a prominent place not only within the specialized genre of military writings but also within the greater canon of Chinese classics.[8] Like all the Chinese classics, the text was analyzed and elaborated upon through the distinctive intellectual vehicle of written commentaries, which not only elucidate but also often extend the insights of the original classical works.[9] The first commentary on *Master Sun's Art of War* was written by one of the most renowned statesmen and strategists in Chinese history, the redoubtable Cao Cao (155–220) of the Han Dynasty, whose commentary has had and continues to have a profound effect on the later reception of the

---

7. For a splendid translation and study of the recently unearthed text, which offers a thorough and revealing account of this issue, see D. C. Lau and Roger T. Ames, *Sun Bin: The Art of Warfare* (New York: Ballantine Books, 1996).

8. For a collection of the most important Chinese military classics, see Ralph D. Sawyer, *The Seven Military Classics of Ancient China* (Boulder, CO: Westview Press, 1993).

9. For a revealing study of this genre and its relationship to the Chinese classics, see John B. Henderson, *Scripture, Canon and Commentary: A Comparison of Confucian and Western Exegesis* (Princeton, NJ: Princeton University Press, 1991).

text.[10] Had Plato written a work on war and Alexander composed a commentary on it, there might have been a similar lineage of influence and elaboration in the West.

Historical Context

In the 1949 film noir *The Third Man*, the character Lime, played by Orson Welles, wryly notes that " . . . in Italy, for thirty years under the Borgias, they had warfare, terror, murder, and bloodshed, but they produced Michelangelo, Leonardo da Vinci, and the Renaissance. In Switzerland, they had brotherly love, they had five hundred years of democracy and peace—and what did that produce—the cuckoo clock." While hardly describing a "law" of history or social development, times of great social strife often do produce remarkable technological and cultural developments. This should not prove too surprising or disturbing, for during such periods people are driven to find new answers to pressing problems, both social and scientific. Societies often muster great resources to support such inquiry and innovation and manage to focus collective attention and energy in unprecedented ways under the pressure of such crises: Necessity often, though not always, is the mother of invention.

Master Sun's Art of War was produced during an age of "warfare, terror, murder, and bloodshed" known as the Warring States Period, the name given to the years covering the latter part of the Eastern Zhou Dynasty (1045–256 BCE) and its aftermath, culminating in the unification of China and the founding of the Qin Dynasty (whence we get the roughly homophonous English word "China") in 221 BCE. The name for this period is taken from the title of a Han Dynasty work, *Record of the Warring States* (*Zhan Guo Ce* 戰國策); it was a time of great strife and considerable suffering, brought about by the decline of the Zhou Dynasty and

---

10. For translations that provide a range of commentaries on the text, see Griffith, *Sun Tzu*, and John Minford, trans., *The Art of War* (London: Penguin Books, 2003). For more on Cao Cao, see Chapter 12, note 2 of this book.

the rise of competition and military conflict among prior vassal states that had become independent of Zhou power and rivals for its throne.

It would please Orson Welles' character Lime to know that the Warring States Period was a time of remarkable creativity and innovation. It saw the proliferation of the so-called age of the "hundred schools" of philosophy: a period of philosophical speculation and diversity unrivaled in human history.[11] It also saw many new and imaginative beliefs and practices concerning human mortality. As the stability and security of the old Zhou order began to wobble and the world seemed to be spinning out of control, people sought new ways to understand and thereby in some sense control the growing chaos that was spreading and enveloping them.[12] One of the direct causes of the growing philosophical and religious skepticism and the general anxiety about life, death, and all that might transpire between and beyond, which marked this age, was the mounting military activity of the Warring States Period. To realize their political ambition of conquering their rival states and unifying all of China, rulers of the Warring States Period increasingly relied upon military "solutions." This encouraged the development of a broad range of the technologies of war and ushered in a new kind of specialized counselor or consultant: experts in military strategy, such as Sunzi.[13]

This period also saw a profound shift in the conception and practice of war. Prior to the Warring States, warfare was more aristocratic and ritualized.[14] Armies were much smaller and their operations were

---

11. For an introduction to the philosophical thought of this period, see Benjamin I. Schwartz, *The World of Thought in Ancient China* (Cambridge, MA: Belknap Press, 1985) and Angus C. Graham, *Disputers of the Tao: Philosophical Argument in Ancient China* (La Salle, IL: Open Court, 1989).

12. For a collection of essays, many of which explore this phenomenon in the philosophical and religious beliefs and practices of this and other periods in Chinese history, see Amy L. Olberding and Philip J. Ivanhoe, eds., *Mortality and Traditional China* (Albany: State University of New York Press, 2011).

13. For evidence internal to the text of this new kind of role, see Chapter I, note 7.

14. David S. Nivison offers a revealing analysis of the relationship between "moral

controlled by aristocrats who observed a kind of chivalric code of conduct even in war. For example, there is a famous story in the *Zuo Commentary* (*Zuozhuan* 左傳) to the *Spring and Autumn Annals* (*Chunqiu* 春秋) that describes how the Duke of Song (宋) engaged a much larger invading force from Chu (楚) in spring 637 BCE.[15] The battle took place on the banks of the Hong (泓) River. The Song army had already crossed over and formed its ranks and was waiting for the advancing force from Chu as they began to ford. Zi Yu 子魚, Song's minister of war, urged the duke to attack immediately, before all of the Chu forces could get across the river. Facing a numerically superior force, Zi Yu wisely counseled this strategy, which would enable the Song to engage a small percentage of the Chu army—those who already had forded the river—while the rest remained mired in the river crossing.[16] The duke, though, rejected his advice. With mounting apprehension and frustration, Zi Yu again urged the duke to attack as soon as the forces from Chu had crossed the river but before they had formed their ranks, hoping at least to take advantage of their disarray. The duke again refused. He held his attack until the enemy had completely forded the river and formed their ranks. The result was a stunning defeat for Song at the hands of the assembled forces of the Chu; the duke himself was wounded in the thigh. Defending his actions, the duke described the older aristocratic ideal of war:[17]

> A gentleman will not inflict a second wound or take gray-haired men as prisoners. He will not take advantage of an

---

charisma" (*de* 德) and military operations in "'Virtue' in Bone and Bronze," in Bryan W. Van Norden, ed., *The Ways of Confucianism: Investigations in Chinese Philosophy* (La Salle, IL: Open Court, 1996), 17–30.

15. For a complete translation of this account, see James Legge, trans., *The Chʻun Tsʻew with the Tso Chuen in The Chinese Classics*, Volume 5, Reprint (Hong Kong: Hong Kong University Press, 1970), 183. The passages below are my translations.

16. Sunzi describes and advocates precisely this strategy in Chapter 9 of our text. Much of his discussion and even his language are similar to this story in the *Spring and Autumn Annals*.

17. For an example of this kind of aristocratic warfare involving archers mounted

enemy making a difficult crossing or narrow passage. While I am but the humble representative of the remnants of a lost state, I will not sound the attack until my enemy has formed his ranks.

In response to this noble and touching declaration, Zi Yu replies, giving voice to the newly emerging attitude toward war:

My lord does not understand war. To have a strong enemy in the middle of a difficult crossing and not yet able to form ranks is a boon bestowed by Heaven. Is it not perfectly permissible to sound the attack while the enemy is at such a disadvantage? What is there to worry about? Moreover, all the strong men who oppose us today are our enemy. We should capture even the very old among them, as long as we can lay hold of them! Why care simply because some have gray hair? The reason we emphasize the notion of shame when we train soldiers for war is because we want them to kill the enemy. If the wound one inflicts is not fatal, why hesitate to strike again? If one forbears wounding a second time, in a way, this is like refraining from wounding at all. If one forbears capturing those with gray hair, in a way, this is like surrendering to them.

Zi Yu describes a more realist conception of war: War was coming to be regarded as a practical task—not a ritual performance—a kind of business, and as the Warring States Period unfolded, business was good. This shift in the conception of warfare occurred alongside a range of remarkable developments in the technology of war.

The Warring States Period witnessed the discovery and proliferation of Iron Age technology, which led to the replacement of the bronze armor, shields, and weapons of prior ages.[18] This period also saw the first use of cavalry, which was deployed alongside the older war chariots

in war chariots, see *Mengzi* (*Mencius*) 4B24.

18. For a highly informative introduction to early Chinese weapons, see Yang Hong, *Weapons in Ancient China* (New York: Science Press, 1992).

used by earlier, aristocratic warriors.[19] War chariots remained the core weapon of early Chinese armies, so much so that the strength of a state was measured in terms of the number of chariots it could field.[20] Chariots were mainstays of the Qin Dynasty's military and continued to be used into the early years of the Western Han Dynasty (206 BCE–24 CE). The longevity of war chariots owed much to their speed, maneuverability, and firepower as well as their suitability for the terrain of northern and central China, the most distinctive feature of which is the sprawling plains surrounding the lower reaches of the Yellow River in the north and the Yangtze River in the south. Four-horse chariots generally carried two or three soldiers, including the driver, and the fighting members of a chariot crew could make use of a large quantity of different weapons. Chariots were also used for command and control by serving as mobile platforms for the banners and drums used to direct troop movements. The use of the chariot evolved over time. For example, in later years, spearheads were added to the ends of both axles as an anti-infantry weapon. These became particularly important as the Warring States Period unfolded and saw the first use of mass infantry; armies of tens or hundreds of thousands of men took the field in increasingly vicious wars of expansion.[21]

Crossbows can be found in China as early as the sixth century BCE, but they were not in widespread use until the middle of the fourth century BCE. Compound bows continued to be used alongside crossbows as each had distinctive tactical advantages. Crossbows had the virtues of long range, devastating penetrating power, low cost, and relatively low levels of skill needed to wield them. Large numbers of crossbow archers could quickly be trained and equipped at modest cost

---

19. The first cavalry units were purportedly deployed in 307 BCE by King Wuling of Zhao. There is no mention of cavalry in *Master Sun's Art of War*, which provides strong evidence of a relatively early date for this work.

20. For example, see *Mengzi* 1A1.

21. For an excellent introduction to warfare in early China, see Mark Edward Lewis, *Sanctioned Violence in Early China* (Albany: State University of New York Press, 1990).

and could produce withering firepower when properly deployed. On the other hand, conventional archers, using compound bows, could sustain higher rates of fire; their weapons were light and easy to handle, which made them indispensible, especially as cavalry became an increasingly important and common feature of Chinese armies.

Infantrymen of the period were lightly armored and carried a variety of weapons and shields. In addition to swords, pikes, spears, and dagger axes (spears with cutting blades) were among the most popular and lethal armaments. With the different states of the period fielding massive armies of chariots, infantry, and later cavalry, armed with an increasingly complex panoply of weapons, armor, and fighting machines—in need of supply, reinforcement, and command and control, and often deployed on distant campaigns for long periods of time—the art of war became increasingly demanding and complex. The nature of warfare in this time required sophisticated logistical systems to raise, train, supply, and control such large forces, maintain them in the field, focus them effectively on their targets and objectives, and lead them decisively to complete their missions and achieve victory. War gave birth not only to a supporting bureaucracy and specialized military experts but also to the arts of organization and strategy, which took shape and in turn influenced the conception, development, and practice of war through works such as *Master Sun's Art of War*.

Prominent Ideas

Master Sun's Art of War presents war as a part of human life. As noted earlier, the text sees conflict as an inevitable feature of life, and when conflict occurs at the level of states, it can manifest itself as war. This reflects a widely seen and still-common idea in Chinese thought and culture concerning the contrasting but complementary notions *wen* 文 ("the cultural") and *wu* 武 ("the martial"). While human societies remain poised and over time alternate between these two states, the Chinese have tended to regard the latter as a kind of deviation, albeit an unavoidable one, from the normal state of human affairs. The ideal is to maintain a state of peace, harmony, and prosperity; war is seen as a perversion of this norm, a temporary phenomenon that we must endure to bring the world back to its proper state. As noted above, this general view may partly explain Sunzi's insistence that military campaigns must be short and decisive.

The lower status of war and those who prosecute it is seen throughout Chinese culture. For example, one prominent and influential classical example of the relative value of civil to military culture is seen in Kongzi's comments about the court music of different ages. Kongzi proclaimed that the highest form of music was the *Shao* 韶, the court music of the legendary sage emperor Shun. We are told of the profound effect this music had upon Kongzi in *Analects* 7.14, "The Master heard the *Shao* in Qi and for three months did not notice the taste of the meat he ate. He said, 'I never dreamt the joys of music could reach such heights!'" Still good but clearly below the *Shao* was the *Wu* 武, the music of a king also named Wu 武 ("martial"), who overthrew the debauched and wicked last ruler of the Shang Dynasty and founded the Zhou Dynasty.[22] In *Analects* 3.25, Kongzi describes the relative virtues of these two kinds of music: "The *Shao* is both perfectly beautiful and perfectly good. The *Wu* is perfectly beautiful but not perfectly good." The difference is that the former music represented an age of peace and harmony, an era of perfect *culture*, while the latter represented an age of righteous conquest or the ideal application of *military* power. In both, the virtues of unity, order, harmony, and moderation were present, but these—particularly the latter two—could only be fully and perfectly expressed in the *Shao* music. This general view of the relative merit of culture over military excellence persists down to the present day in China; military achievements, while appreciated, are still regarded as far inferior to cultural achievements. A common Chinese expression teaches "Good iron is not made into nails; good men do not become soldiers" (hao tie bu wei ding; hao ren bu wei bing 好鐵不為釘; 好人不為兵). Such a sentiment is diametrically opposed to what one finds in modern recruiting slogans such as "The Marine Corps builds

---

22. For these and other early dynasties, see Chapter 13, note 5.

men" or "The Marines are looking for a few good men."[23] Despite the experience of war, revolution, and the adulation of Mao Zedong, it is important to appreciate that in general, military experience is not highly valued among contemporary Chinese people. It plays almost no part in views or arguments about who is best qualified to lead the country, a stark contrast to cultures such as the United States, where prior military service is almost always a strong advantage in races for political office. This attitude further distinguishes Chinese views on war and political leadership from an idea found in Machiavelli but made famous by Clausewitz: that war is simply the *extension* of politics by other means.[24]

Master Sun's Art of War retains the general Chinese tendency to regard war as an unfortunate departure from life's proper work, but it faces this threat squarely and treats the conduct of war as a practical problem. In so doing, it breaks with an older, highly moralized view of not only the justifications for war, but also its conduct and proper postbellum behavior, which can be found in earlier thinkers, such as Kongzi and his followers.[25] In this respect, *Master Sun's Art of War* is very much a product of its age. Unfortunately for humankind, war has remained a persistent intrusion disturbing and often destroying periods of peace, harmony, and prosperity. The traditional Chinese view of alternating phases of

---

23. While both of these are modern recruiting slogans, the latter incorporates a phrase of venerable origin. "A few good men" is taken from an advertisement by Captain William Jones, who sought "a few good men" to join him aboard the frigate *Providence*. See Edwin H. Simmons, *The United States Marines: A History* (Annapolis, MD: Naval Institute Press, 1998), 17.

24. While widely attributed to Clausewitz, this is one proposition in a dialectical argument he entertains and not a claim he seeks to establish or defend.

25. The Confucian perspective on the ethics of war continues to play a vital role in both policy formation and everyday discourse about war. For example, many Chinese criticized the second Gulf War by invoking arguments drawn from early Confucian texts. For two contemporary accounts of Confucian views on the ethics of war, see Daniel A. Bell, "Just War and Confucianism: Implications for the Contemporary World," in *Beyond Liberal Democracy: Political Thinking for an East Asian Context* (Princeton, NJ: Princeton University Press, 2006), 23–51, and Yu Kam-por, "Confucian Views on War as Seen in the *Gongyang Commentary on the Spring and Autumn Annals*," *DAO: A Journal of Comparative Philosophy* 9, no. 1 (2010): 97–111.

peace and war ("the cultural" and "the martial") accurately portrays a recurring, yet regrettable, theme in human history. In this respect, *Master Sun's Art of War*, while a product of its age, continues to teach lessons in and for our own time.

In modern conceptions of warfare, "shaping the battle space" refers to the general aim of molding situations on the battlefield in ways that offer military advantage to the commander. *Master Sun's Art of War* contains many passages concerned with this topic and the bulk of Chapters 4 through 6 is focused on what modern tacticians call battle-space shaping. Sunzi uses his own distinctive terms of art to describe different ways to shape the battle space. The title of Chapter 4 is "Disposition of Forces," or *xing* 形, and the basic meaning of this Chinese term is "shape" or "form." The chapter concerns different postures, deployments, and temperaments that go into successful military campaigns. Another theme of this chapter, and one seen throughout the text, is the idea that mastering strategy requires engaging in a kind of self-cultivation: One must master oneself as well as the lessons of war if one seeks to travel the path to victory. The character and attitudes a general brings to conflict are as important as the troops and equipment he can muster and can be equally decisive in determining the outcome of a battle or war. Chapter 5 is titled "Strategic Potential" (*shi* 勢), which is a complex and slippery notion in early Chinese philosophy and strategy.[26] The basic idea is that there is a hidden structure and potential within every situation or condition which can be brought into play and directed to one's advantage. The modern notion of a tipping point offers one illustration of strategic potential at work, as does the idea that finding and knocking out the keystone can bring a large edifice crumbling to the ground. Sunzi's interest in strategic potential is focused on ways in which good planning can bring into play inherent powers on the battlefield that the astute general can use to decisive advantage. The title of Chapter 6, "Tenuousness and Solidity"

---

26. For a thorough and revealing analysis of this idea in both military and political contexts, see Roger T. Ames, *The Art of Rulership: A Study of Ancient Chinese Political Thought* (Albany: State University of New York Press, 1994), 65–107.

(*xu shi* 虛實), takes up two terms from the broader philosophical discourse of early China and applies them to the arena of war. These paired characters offer a rich spectrum of contrasting yet complementary ideas. The most basic contrast is between things that are amorphous, unformed, and indistinct (*xu*) and those that are solid, set, and clearly seen (*shi*). Of course, Sunzi is interested in how these ideas play out on the battlefield. One way they do so is by showing that under certain conditions there is greater strength in tenuousness. If one's forces cannot be seen clearly or if one's lines easily yield to an enemy's probing, only to lure him into a devastating and unexpected encounter, the apparent weakness of being tenuous can lead to victory over what is stable, firm, and "solid." Another variation on these related themes is that what is tenuous can come together, thereby suddenly giving rise to a massive wall of "solidity." Minute drops of water can pool together, rise, and come crashing down as a mighty wave; even the most amorphous and tenuous wisps of breeze can gather into a violent and destructive storm. In an analogous way, widely scattered troops, which present the enemy with an apparently weak and "tenuous" line of defense, can be drawn together quickly into a "solid" mass of humanity and deliver a crushing blow. Sunzi explores the notions of tenuousness and solidity and their implication for the use of military force with the aim of victory in battle.

This brief Introduction cannot possibly do justice to the full range of complex and profound ideas contained in *Master Sun's Art of War*. As noted earlier, the text has generated an extremely long and rich tradition of commentary, which continues to be added to in modern times, as this venerable classic continues to invoke and inspire insights in generations of readers.

Conclusion

Pace Protagoras, man is not the measure of all things; but he was close: We are the *measurers* of all things. If we are wise, among the most important things we measure are ourselves and in war human beings are afforded a unique opportunity to take the measure of who and what they are, for better and for worse. War threatens not just individuals but society as a whole, and under such conditions people display uncharacteristic levels of diligence, creativity, cooperation, and sacrifice; they also display some of their most vile and vicious tendencies toward one another, other creatures, and the world at large. Because of this, the wise follow Master Sunzi's counsel concerning war: "One cannot fail to investigate and study it."

The activity of war presents human beings with a unique opportunity to display both virtue and vice. While courage is by no means limited to the context of war, this virtue finds many of its clearest and most poignant examples in acts of physical heroism upon the field of battle. In such circumstances, great risk and ultimate sacrifice are the norm and consequences regularly are direct, clear, and dramatic. Classic accounts of courage, such as Aristotle's, describe it almost exclusively as a martial virtue.[27] Vice is the dark, cold shadow of virtue; traits such as cruelty are not strangers to the battlefield and the concept of cruelty itself is challenged within the crucible of war, where hard choices are part of life and the timid, kind, and hesitant cannot survive.

Because war involves life and death and stands as the epitome of conflict, it often is invoked as a metaphor for other types of competition and struggle, and its particular characteristics and qualities enrich our ability to understand and express important features of these other dimensions of human life. People talk of economic or athletic competition as "battles" or "wars," and much can be learned and made clear by such comparisons. Like war, these activities involve sometimes fierce competition, require focused effort and sacrifice, and often result in clear winners and losers. On the other hand, while helpful in capturing certain critical features of economic or athletic activity, the metaphor of war also can distort or warp our view of these aspects of human life.

---

27. The early Confucian philosopher Mengzi (Mencius) also presented an insightful analysis of courage drawing upon military examples. For a study of this issue, see my "Mengzi's Conception of Courage" in *DAO: A Journal of Comparative Philosophy*, special issue edited by Xiao Yang, 5, no. 2 (2006): 221–34.

For unlike war, where death and destruction are constituent parts of the activity, economic or athletic competition does not require and almost never involves killing, mutilation, or widespread devastation. Invoking the metaphor of war in regard to such activities expresses not only the depth of our commitment to winning such competitions, but it also exaggerates the extent to which we are prepared or permitted to go and can distort the nature of such endeavors.

The notion of a "war on poverty" offers another excellent example of the metaphor of war; the primary characteristic being invoked is the all-out commitment typical of and required by war and perhaps also a sense of the degree to which we loathe the target of our ire and effort. We see similar features in other cases in which people describe a goal or commitment as "the moral equivalent of war."[28] The ongoing "battle to defeat cancer" implies all of the ideas mentioned above but adds the imminent threat of death and the corresponding hope of conquest and survival. The depth and intensity of our commitment, as well as the degree to which people selectively invoke the characteristics of war, also are clearly on display when we talk of love as a "war" or "battle" between the sexes and recognize that in such contexts there can be a thin line between love and hate. Such metaphorical uses of the concept of war can be worked to express further insight and nuance, as when Henry Kissinger noted, "Nobody will ever win the Battle of the Sexes. There's just too much fraternizing with the enemy."

In all these examples, we see how pervasive a number of the essential features of war are in human life in general. Many other activities are forms of competition or struggle, call on us to make commitments and sacrifices, stir and focus intense feelings of love and hate,

---

28. The expression "the moral equivalent of war" was coined by William James, and is the title of an essay he wrote in 1910, which helped to inspire such movements as the Civilian Conservation Corps in the 1930s and the Peace Corps in the 1960s. See the introduction by John McDermott to *Essays in Religion and Morality, Volume 11 of The Works of William James* (Cambridge, MA: Harvard University Press, 1982), xxv–xxvi; the essay itself is found on pp. 162–73 of that work. Thanks to Michael R. Slater for pointing out that James was the author of this expression and for explaining its later influence.

and require understanding not only our opponents but also ourselves. Sunzi expresses this last point in a particularly elegant and well-known line, "Know your enemy and yourself and through a hundred battles you will never be in danger."[29] The aspects of war described above help to explain why interest in *Master Sun's Art of War* has never been confined to professional soldiers and others interested and involved in the work of war. It concerns issues that range far beyond the battlefield that, in fact, are unavoidable features of human life, and as a result it continues to find a broad and diverse audience. Mao Zedong's writings on warfare are a part of Sunzi's legacy as are contemporary discussions of his work among military strategists, businesspeople, and practitioners of Chinese chess (*weiqi* 圍棋)[30] around the world. Like all classic works, *Master Sun's Art of War* has no simple set of lessons to teach or any definitive interpretation. It presents a collection of stimulating topics, themes, and ideas, opens up paths for reflection and further inquiry, and invites readers to take these up into their own imaginations, thoughts, actions, and lives to rediscover and create new insights about the shifting, elusive, threatening, and yet seductively exhilarating phenomena surrounding conflict and how to respond to it successfully.

---

29. See Chapter 3.

30. Known in Japan as *go* 碁 and in Korea as *baduk* 바둑.

Master Sun's
Art of War

Chapter 1

Assessing[1]

計

Master Sun said,

"War is a major affair of state, the ground of life or death, the way of preservation or oblivion. One cannot fail to investigate and study it. And so,[2] manage it according to five concerns, and carry out a comparative assessment between yourself and your enemy, in order to investigate and study how things really stand.

The first concern is ethics,

The second concern is weather,[3]

The third concern is terrain,

The fourth concern is leadership,

The fifth concern is methods.

By 'ethics' I mean what leads the people to agree with their superior and persuades them to follow him in life or death without fearing

計

any danger.[4] By 'weather' I mean *yin* and *yang*,[5] hot and cold, and the alternation of the seasons. By 'terrain'[6] I mean the distance or nearness to be traversed, the difficulty or ease of passage, the openness or narrowness for maneuver, and how these are conducive to life or death. By 'leadership' I mean wisdom, trustworthiness, care, courage, and discipline. By 'methods' I mean organizational structure, command and control, and the proper use of supplies. Every general is familiar with these five concerns. Those who understand them are victorious; those who fail to understand them are not.

"And so, carry out a comparative assessment between yourself and your enemy in regard to these, in order to discover how things really stand.

Which general is ethical?

Which ruler has ability?

Who enjoys the advantages of weather and terrain?

Whose methods and orders are carried out?

Who has the strongest troops?

Whose soldiers are well trained?

Who follows an enlightened policy of reward and promotion?

By assessing these concerns, I know who will win and who will lose. If the ruler listens to my plans and employs me, he shall win, and so I shall stay. If the ruler does not listen to my advice, even though he employs me, he will be defeated, and so I shall leave.[7]

"Once you have heard a proper assessment of who has what advantages, you must work to harness strategic potential,[8] in order to draw upon and augment your advantages. Strategic potential allows you to make use of your advantages in order to control the flow of power.

"The way of war is deception. And so, when you have the ability to strike, appear as if you have none. When busy deploying your troops and equipment, appear unengaged. When you are near, appear far away. When far away, appear near. Use the prospect of advantage to lure the enemy in. If they are chaotic and confused, seize them. If they are solid and secure, prepare for them. If they are strong, avoid them. If they are angry, irritate them. If they are mean and cowardly, encourage them to be arrogant and haughty. If they are resting, harry them. If they are united, divide them. Attack whenever they are ill prepared. Appear where they least expect

計

it. This is how the enlightened warrior wins victory; it is not something that can be taught prior to knowing how to prepare for war.

"Prior to battle, carry out a proper assessment in one's ancestral temple.[9] Those with the most factors in their favor shall win. Those with the fewest factors in their favor shall lose. How much poorer the prospects of those who have *no* factors in their favor!

"When I look at things in this way, it is easy to see who will win."

Chapter 2

Waging War

Master Sun said,

"Whenever you deploy an army, you need:

> One thousand fighting chariots,
>
> One thousand light and heavy wagons,
>
> One hundred thousand armored infantrymen,
>
> And enough provisions to support troops stationed more than one thousand leagues away.[1]

"In addition, there are:

> In-country and foreign expenditures,
>
> Funds for entertaining envoys,
>
> Materials needed for repairs,
>
> Maintenance for vehicles and armor.

"The cost for all this is one thousand pieces of

gold per day. Only once adequate funds are in hand can one raise an army of one hundred thousand men.

"The aim of war is victory. When war is drawn out and prolonged, troops become dull and lose their edge. Attacking cities uses up their strength. If you keep the army in the field for long periods of time, the resources of the state will prove insufficient. If troops become dull and lose their edge, their strength will be depleted and supplies will be exhausted; the feudal lords will take advantage of such weaknesses and rise up. Then, even the wisest will not be able to deal with the consequences.

"And so, I have heard that even the most inept general seeks swift victory but have never seen a skillful general draw out a conflict. There has never been a case of a state benefiting from a protracted war.

"And so, one who does not thoroughly understand what can harm the waging of war cannot thoroughly understand what can benefit it.

"Those good at deploying an army do not seek a second round of conscription or a third round of provisioning.[2] They bring the tools of war from their own country but feed off their enemies. In this way, their troops always have enough to eat.

"A state is impoverished by its army when it must send supplies over great distances. When supplies are sent over great distances, the common people are made poor. Prices are high when an army is nearby. When prices are high, the common people's supply of goods is depleted. When the common people's supply of goods is depleted, they become anxious about paying military levies. Their strength exhausted, their goods depleted, the homes of the state are emptied of wealth. In this way, the common people lose seven-tenths of what they own, while the court loses six-tenths of what it owns—having to pay for damaged carts, spent horses, armor, helmets, arrows, crossbows, lances, light and heavy shields, draft oxen, and supply wagons.

"And so, the wise general works to feed off his enemy. One bushel of the enemy's food is worth twenty sent from home. One bale of the enemy's fodder is worth twenty sent from home.

"Now, soldiers kill their enemies out of anger but plunder their goods because of the prospect of reward. And so, whenever more than ten enemy chariots are captured, reward the soldier who captured the first. Replace the flags and banners of the captured chariots with your own, mix these vehicles among your ranks, and assign them crews. Treat prisoners of war well and take care of them. This is known as 'defeating the enemy while adding to one's own strength.'[3]

"And so, in war the important thing is victory, not prolonged conflict. A general who understands war is the arbiter of life and death for the people and minister of security or peril for the state."

Chapter 3

Offensive Strategy

Master Sun said,

"Whenever you deploy an army: It is best to capture an intact state; capturing a destroyed state is less good. It is best to capture an intact army; capturing a destroyed army is less good. It is best to capture an intact battalion; capturing a destroyed battalion is less good. It is best to capture an intact company; capturing a destroyed company is less good. It is best to capture an intact squad; capturing a destroyed squad is less good.

"And so, to prove victorious in every battle is not the best possible outcome. The best possible outcome is to subdue the enemy's troops *without* fighting.

"In military operations, it is best to attack the enemy's strategy.

謀
攻

Next best is to attack the enemy's alliances.

Next best is to attack the enemy's troops.

Worst of all is to lay siege to the enemy's cities.

"Laying siege to the enemy's cities should be undertaken only as a last resort. Preparing protective covers and armored assault vehicles requires three months' time. Making ready the necessary siege weapons takes another three months. Constructing siege ramps requires another three months of work.

"An impatient general, unable to control his anger, sends his troops scurrying up the city walls like ants, ensuring that one in three shall die, even though the city does not fall. This is the kind of disaster that comes from such attacks.

"And so, one who is good at conducting military operations subdues the enemy's troops without fighting, captures the enemy's cities without laying siege to them, and defeats the enemy's state without having to engage in a protracted campaign.

"Whenever you engage in a conflict, always employ a comprehensive plan. Then, your troops will not be worn down and your advantage will be complete. This is the method of offensive strategy.

"And so, whenever you engage in military operations, if you enjoy a ten-to-one advantage over the enemy, surround them. If you enjoy a five-to-one advantage, attack them. If you enjoy a two-to-one advantage, divide their forces. If you are equal in strength, engage them in battle. If you are inferior in number, elude them. If you are in no way your enemy's match, avoid contact. A small force tenaciously resisting will be captured by a large force.

"The general is a mainstay of the state. If the mainstay is solid, the state will be strong. If the mainstay is defective, the state will be weak.

"There are three ways in which a ruler can bring trouble to his army: First, if he orders an advance without knowing that the army cannot advance or orders a retreat without knowing that the army cannot retreat—this is known as 'hobbling the army.' Second, if he joins in the administration of the military even though he is unfamiliar with military affairs, this will cause confusion among officers and troops. Third, if he joins in the supervision of the army even though he is unfamiliar with military command, this will sow confusion

謀
攻

and doubt among officers and troops. When there is confusion and doubt among officers and troops, this will encourage the feudal lords to cause problems. This is known as 'sowing chaos in the ranks and turning away from victory.'

"There are five ways to know whether you will be victorious: If you know when to fight and when not to fight, you will be victorious. If you understand how to use both large and small forces, you will be victorious. If those above and those below desire the same ends, you will be victorious. If you wait well prepared for those who are ill prepared, you will be victorious. If your general is capable and the ruler does not interfere with him, you will be victorious. These five are the ways to know whether you will be victorious.

"And so, it is said, 'Know your enemy and yourself and through a hundred battles you will never be in danger. If you do not know your enemy but only know yourself, you will lose as many battles as you win. If you know neither your enemy nor yourself, in every battle you will be in danger.'"

Chapter 4

Disposition of Forces

Master Sun said,

"In the past, those good at waging war first made themselves invincible and then waited for the enemy to leave themselves vulnerable. Being invincible is something that lies within one's own power to achieve, being vulnerable is something the enemy determines. And so, good warriors are able to make themselves invincible but are not able to make the enemy vulnerable. This is why it is said, 'Victory is something you can know how to achieve but not something you can guarantee.'

"Against an invincible foe, take up a defensive posture. Against a vulnerable foe, go on the attack. Defend when your forces are inadequate. Attack when your forces are abundant.

"Those good at defense hide within the deepest layers of the earth. Those good at attack

形

move across the highest reaches of heaven. In this way, they are able to protect themselves and complete their victories.

"To see victory when everyone knows that victory is at hand is not the height of achievement. To be victorious in battle and have the whole world proclaim how good you are is not the height of achievement. It does not take great strength to lift an autumn hair.[1] It does not take keen eyes to see the sun or the moon. It does not take sharp ears to hear the clapping of thunder.

"In ancient times, those known for being good at waging war were victorious over those easy to defeat.[2] And so, the victories of those good at waging war do not bring them fame for sagacity or merit for courage. The victories of such warriors are flawless. Those who are flawless are certain to attain victory in any endeavor they undertake. They achieve victory over those who already are defeated.

"And so, those good at waging war take up an invincible position and never allow the enemy any chance to evade defeat. In this way, a victorious army first assures victory and then seeks to do battle. A losing army first engages in battle and then seeks for victory.

"Those good at military operations cultivate the way described above and stick to proper methods. These are the methods of warfare:

First, there is measurement.

Second, there is weighing.

Third, there is calculation.

Fourth, there is balancing.

Fifth, there is gauging the likelihood of victory.

Terrain gives rise to measurement.

Measurement gives rise to weighing.

Weighing gives rise to calculation.

Calculation gives rise to balancing.

Balancing gives rise to gauging the likelihood of victory.

"And so, a victorious army is like a pound weighed against a grain. A defeated army is like a grain weighed against a pound.[3] The reason a victorious army fights like a flood of water released from a reservoir a thousand fathoms deep is owing to the disposition of its forces."

Chapter 5

Strategic Potential

Master Sun said,

"The key to managing a large number of troops is the same as managing a small number: organization and assignments. The key to commanding a large number of troops is the same as commanding a small number: signals and orders. The key to ensuring that the army can engage the enemy without ever suffering defeat is the use of regular and special forces.[1] The key to ensuring that the application of military force is as decisive as throwing a grindstone onto an egg is understanding tenuousness and solidity.[2]

"Always use regular forces to engage the enemy and special forces to defeat them. The tactics of those who are good at deploying special forces are as infinite as heaven and earth and as inexhaustible as the mightiest rivers. They wane only to wax full again, like the sun or the

勢

moon. They pass away only to be reborn, like the progression of the four seasons. There are only five notes, but these can produce an inexhaustible variety of sounds.[3] There are only five colors, but these can produce an inexhaustible variety of hues.[4] There are only five tastes, but these can produce an inexhaustible variety of flavors.[5] Regular and special forces offer the only strategic potentials for battle,[6] but their permutations and combinations are infinite and inexhaustible. Regular and special forces give rise to one another: like a turning circle, they have no beginning or end. Who could possibly exhaust them?

"The swiftness of a rushing torrent can float boulders; this is a matter of the water's strategic potential.[7] The swiftness of a diving hawk can break the back of its prey; this is a matter of the hawk's precise timing. And so, those good at waging war unleash overwhelming strategic potential and employ precise timing. Strategic potential is like a drawn crossbow. Timing is like pulling the trigger.

"Amidst the clash and clamor of the most chaotic battle, their troops cannot be disrupted. Turning and circling in endlessly complex formations, they can never be defeated.

Order can give rise to chaos.

Courage can give rise to cowardice.

Strength can give rise to weakness.

Whether there is order or chaos depends on proper organization and assignments. Whether there is courage or cowardice depends on strategic potential. Whether there is strength or weakness depends on the disposition of one's forces.

"And so, those good at moving the enemy:

> When they display a certain disposition of forces, the enemy is sure to follow. When they make a certain offering, the enemy is sure to accept. Move the enemy with the prospect of gain. Lie in wait for them with your forces at the ready.

"Those good at waging war look to strategic potential and do not simply rely on the strength of individuals. They select the right people and then trust in strategic potential. Those who trust in strategic potential use their troops in the way one rolls logs or stones. It is in the nature of logs and stones to be at rest when on flat ground but in motion when on a precipitous slope, to stay put when squared off but to roll when rounded. And so, the strategic

potential of those who are good at waging war
is like rolling logs and stones off the side of a
mountain a thousand fathoms high—such is
the nature of strategic potential!"

Chapter 6

Tenuousness and Solidity[1]

Master Sun said,

"Those who are first to take the field of battle and wait for the enemy are at ease. Those who are last to take the field of battle and must rush into battle are worn out and weary. And so, those good at waging war manipulate the enemy and are not manipulated by them. Encourage the enemy to arrive by offering them advantages. Prevent the enemy from arriving by causing them harm.

When they are at ease, find a way to wear them out.

When they are full, find a way to starve them.

When they are at rest, find a way to move them.

虚
實

Appear in places they cannot move to swiftly.

Move swiftly to places they do not expect you to go.

"Those who march a thousand leagues without being weary march where there are no enemies to encounter.

"Those who always succeed in taking their objectives attack what is not defended. Those who always succeed in defending their positions defend what is not attacked. And so, those good at launching an attack ensure the enemy does not know what to defend. Those good at defending their positions ensure the enemy does not know what to attack.

"So subtle! So subtle!

They are without form.[2]

So spirit-like! So spirit-like!

They make no sound.

And so, the enemy's fate lies in their hands.

"Those who advance and cannot be repelled assault the tenuous places in the enemy's defenses. Those who withdraw and cannot be pursued move too swiftly to be caught.

"And so, when I desire to join battle, even if the enemy is secure behind high walls and surrounded by a deep moat, they still must engage me, because I attack a place they must relieve and reinforce.[3] When I do not desire to join battle, even if all I do is draw a circle on the ground as my line of defense, the enemy still cannot engage me, because I misdirect and mislead their forces far afield.

"And so, I cause the enemy to reveal the disposition of their forces, but mine remains invisible; my forces remain unified while the enemy must split up to search for me. My forces are one; the enemy is divided into many smaller units. This allows me to focus all of my forces to attack a small fraction of theirs and enjoy decisive numerical superiority. If you are able to attack a small force with a much larger force, the unit you choose to attack will find itself in desperate straits.

"I cannot let the enemy know where I will choose to attack. If they do not know where I will attack, they must prepare for attack in many places. The enemy must prepare for attack in many places, but I will choose to attack only a few. And so, if the enemy prepares their front lines, they will have few troops at the rear. If they prepare their rear lines, they will have few

虚
實

troops at the front. If they prepare their left flank, they will have few troops on the right. If they prepare their right flank, they will have few troops on the left. If they prepare on all fronts, then they will have few troops on all fronts.

Numerical inferiority results from being forced to prepare for the enemy's attack. Numerical superiority results from forcing the enemy to prepare for your attack.

"And so, if you know where and when the battle will be fought, you can join battle even after having marched a thousand leagues. If you do not know where or when the battle will be fought, then your left flank cannot reinforce your right; your right flank cannot reinforce your left; your front cannot reinforce your rear; your rear cannot reinforce your front. How much more difficult would this be for units separated by tens of leagues or even just a few!

"In my view, although Yue has many troops, what benefit is this to determining victory or defeat?[4] And so it is said, 'Victory is something you can craft and bring into being.' Although the enemy enjoys numerical superiority, you can ensure you never have to face their full strength.

Chapter 6
Tenuousness and Solidity

"And so, analyze the enemy in order to understand the strengths and weaknesses of their plans. Provoke the enemy in order to discover their principles of operation. Ascertain the enemy's disposition of forces in order to know the shape of the field of battle. Probe the enemy in order to know where their strength is deficient or abundant.

"The ultimate disposition of forces is for them to have no discernable shape or form.[5] If your forces are without discernable shape or form, then even the most deeply embedded spy cannot ferret them out, even the wisest strategist cannot make plans against them.

"Even though I reveal to the masses the disposition of forces I use in order to achieve victory, they still will not understand how I do it. They all can understand the disposition of forces I use to achieve victory, but none can understand how I control the disposition of forces in order to achieve victory. And so, I never repeat the ways in which I achieve victory; I respond to the infinite variety of ways in which forces can be disposed.

"The disposition of your forces should be like water. Water avoids high ground and rushes to low. An army should avoid substantial enemy forces and strike where the enemy's lines are tenuous. Water adapts to the terrain and allows the land to determine its course. An army should adapt to the disposition of enemy forces and allow this to guide them to victory.

"And so, the strategic potential of an army has no fixed course or expression; just as water has no fixed disposition or form.[6] Those able to achieve victory by changing and transforming in response to the disposition of their enemies are called 'spirit-like.'[7]

"None of the five phases always dominates.[8] None of the four seasons is always in force. Days grow longer or shorter. The moon waxes and wanes."

Chapter 7

The Clash of Arms

Master Sun said,

"Whenever you deploy an army: The general receives his orders from the ruler, assembles the army, mobilizes the masses, and sets up camp near the enemy. The real challenge, though, lies in the clash of arms. What is difficult about the clash of arms is to make the indirect route the most direct and turn misfortune to your advantage.

"And so, travel the indirect route but lure the enemy astray with the prospect of advantage. In this way, you can set off after they depart but arrive before them. This is to understand the strategy of making the indirect route the most direct.

"The clash of arms can lead to advantage; it can also lead to danger. If you throw your entire force into the fray seeking advantage, you will

軍
爭

not attain it.[1] If you rush into the fray with your fastest and most mobile units, seeking advantage, you must abandon your equipment and supply wagons. If, seeking advantage, you order your troops to roll up and store away their armor and set out on a forced march of a hundred leagues,[2] moving day and night without making camp, at a double-time pace, and with only half the number of breaks, all your generals will be captured. This is because your fittest troops will arrive early and your less-fit troops late, providing only one-tenth of your total force for your initial engagement with the enemy. If your forced march covers a distance of fifty leagues, the general of your vanguard force will suffer defeat, because you will have only half of your total force for your initial engagement with the enemy. If your forced march covers a distance of thirty leagues, only two-thirds of your total force will arrive and be ready to engage the enemy.[3]

"And so, an army without equipment and supply wagons will be destroyed. An army without rations and fodder will be destroyed. An army without stores and provisions will be destroyed.

"If you do not know the intentions of the feudal lords, you cannot prepare to make alliances with them. If you do not know the lay of the land—where the mountains, forests, cliffs and slopes, swamps and marshes lie—you cannot march your troops. If you do not avail yourself of local guides, you cannot gain the advantages of the terrain.

"War is founded upon deception, animated by the prospect of advantage, and varies as a result of dividing and assembling.

Be swift as a gust of wind,

Sedate as a forest,

Aggressive as a roaring fire,

Immovable as a mountain,

As difficult to know as *yin*,[4]

As startling as a clap of thunder.

When you plunder a territory, distribute the spoils among your troops. When you expand your territory, distribute the profit. Weigh things carefully and then act. Those who begin by understanding the strategy of how to make the indirect route the most direct shall be victorious. This is the proper method concerning the clash of arms.

"The *Administration of the Army*[5] says, 'In the chaos

軍
爭

and tumult of battle, words cannot be heard, and so one uses gongs and drums. Gestures cannot be seen, and so one uses banners and flags.' Gongs, drums, banners, and flags are means to unify the ears and eyes of your troops. Once your troops are unified, the courageous will not advance on their own and the timid will not retreat on their own. This is the proper method for managing a large number of troops. For night operations, use a large number of signal fires and drums. For daylight operations, use a large number of banners and flags. In this way you can train the ears and eyes of your troops.

"An army can have its fighting spirit taken away from it. A general can have his heart and mind taken away from him.[6]

"Fighting spirit is sharpest in the morning, weakens by midday, and retreats by evening. Those good at waging war avoid engaging when the enemy's fighting spirit is sharp and strike when it is weakening or in retreat. —This is how to manage fighting spirit.

"In good order, await those in chaos. In serenity, await those who are agitated. —This is how to manage heart and mind.

"With those who have come from nearby, wait for those who have come from afar. At ease, wait for those who are weary. With stomach full, wait for those who are hungry. —This is how to manage physical strength.

"Do not engage an enemy advancing under well-ordered flags. Do not strike an enemy with perfectly formed ranks. —This is how to manage variations encountered in the heat of battle.

"These are the proper methods for engaging in battle:

>   Do not assault an enemy on high ground.

>   Do not confront an enemy with their backs to a hill.

>   Do not pursue an enemy who feigns flight.

>   Do not attack troops brimming with fighting spirit.

>   Do not swallow bait the enemy may offer.

>   Do not block an army returning home.

>   Do not fail to leave a surrounded army a way out.[7]

>   Do not press an enemy at bay.

These are the proper methods for engaging in battle."

Chapter 8

Nine Variations

Master Sun said,

"Whenever you deploy an army: The general receives his orders from the ruler, assembles the army, and mobilizes the masses.[1] He does not make camp on difficult or unsuitable terrain. He joins with allies on terrain that offers easy access in every direction. He does not linger on terrain that is desolate or remote. He makes careful plans when occupying terrain that is easy to surround. He fights when on deadly terrain.[2]

"There are roads he does not take. Armies he does not attack. Cities he does not lay siege to. Terrain he will not fight on. And orders he will not accept.

"And so, a general who thoroughly understands the advantages associated with the nine varieties of terrain[3] knows how to deploy an army. A general who does not thoroughly understand the advantages associated with the nine varieties of terrain will not be able to enjoy what these offer, even though he is familiar with the lay of the land. A general who does not understand the art of the nine varieties of terrain will not be able to deploy his forces effectively, even though he is familiar with the five types of advantage.[4]

"Those who are wise consider both advantages and disadvantages. By considering what is advantageous and working toward it, they assure success. By considering what is disadvantageous and being concerned about it, they avoid harm.

"Deter the feudal lords by causing them to suffer disadvantage. Employ the feudal lords by giving them various tasks. Encourage the feudal lords by offering them the chance to enjoy advantages.

"The proper method to deploy an army is not to assume the enemy will not appear but rather to be prepared for their coming; it is not to assume the enemy will not attack but rather to make yourself invincible to their attack.

"There are five dangerous traits a general may have:

> If rash, he can be killed.

> If cowardly, he can be captured.

> If prone to anger, he can be provoked.

> If honest and pure, he can be insulted.

> If tenderhearted, he can be filled with anxiety.

All five of these are faults in a general and a disaster for an army. When an army is defeated and its general killed, the cause can be traced to these five dangerous traits. This is something one cannot fail to investigate and study."

Chapter 9

Maneuvering Forces

Master Sun said,

"Whenever you deploy your troops and prepare to confront the enemy: When crossing mountain ranges, camp in the valleys. Take up positions on high ground, facing south.[1] When battling in higher elevations, never attack uphill. This is the way to deploy your troops in the mountains.

"After fording a body of water, put some distance between your troops and the water.[2] When the enemy is fording a body of water and advancing toward you, don't engage them in the water; it is most advantageous to wait until half their force has crossed over and then strike.[3] If you want to do battle with the enemy, don't engage them near the water's edge. Take up positions on high ground, facing south. Never attack upstream. This is the way to deploy your troops in or near bodies of water.

行
軍

"When crossing swamps or marshes, do so at the utmost speed and never linger. If you engage the enemy in swamps or marshes, be sure to take up positions near fresh water and grass and with an ample number of trees at your back.[4] This is the way to deploy your troops in swamps or marshes.

"On level ground take up positions that afford ease of maneuver and with high ground to your right and back, keeping death in front and life to the rear.[5] This is the way to deploy your troops on level ground.

"The advantages afforded by these four ways of deploying troops enabled the Yellow Emperor to defeat his enemies in all the four directions.[6]

"An army prefers occupying high ground and dislikes being in a lower position. It prizes light and warmth and shuns darkness and cold. It nurtures its life and ensures it is well supplied. When an army avoids illness and remains healthy it is invincible. On mounds or hills, dikes or embankments, take up positions facing south with high ground to your right and back. These are ways in which the terrain can offer your forces an advantage.

Chapter 9
Maneuvering Forces

"When rain falling upstream surges down to your area, wait until the water subsides before attempting to ford.

"If an area contains precipitous gorges, natural wells, natural prisons, natural nets, natural traps, or natural fissures,[7] pass through it quickly and don't go near these features. Distance yourself from these and cause the enemy to get close to them. Keep these in front of you and cause the enemy to have them at their back.

"When marching through areas with treacherous drop-offs, pools and wells, reeds and rushes, forested mountains, or tangled undergrowth, you must carefully scout and reconnoiter them, for these are perfect places to lay ambushes.

"If the enemy is nearby but not moving, they are relying on some treachery. If the enemy is far away but calling you to battle, they are trying to force you to advance. If they occupy a position that affords ease of maneuver, this offers them an advantage.

"When you see many trees swaying in the distance, the enemy is advancing.[8] When you discover obstacles in the thick grass, the enemy is seeking to sow uncertainty among your ranks. If birds suddenly take flight, there will be an

行
軍

ambush. If animals are startled and stampede, there will be a surprise attack. If you see high, narrow columns of dust in the distance, chariots are approaching. If the dust clouds are low and spread out, infantry is on the way. If the dust clouds are scattered and arrive intermittently, the enemy is gathering firewood. If the dust clouds are few and seem to come and go, they are making camp.

"If the enemy sends envoys who speak humbly while their forces continue to make preparations, they are about to advance. If their envoys speak forcefully while their forces launch a sudden advance, they are about to retreat. If the enemy's light chariots are first to take the field and line up on the flanks, they are about to form ranks. If, without prior consultation, the enemy seeks a truce, they are plotting something. If their soldiers march at the double time and parade their war chariots about, they are waiting for something. If half their forces advance while the other half retreat, they are seeking to lure you out. If their troops lean on their weapons when they stand, they are short of food. If their troops drink before drawing their ration, they are short of water. If the enemy sees an advantage but does not advance to seize it, they are weary. If birds gather above their camp, their ranks are thinning. If their men call out in the night, they have lost their nerve. If their troops are disorderly, they no longer take their general seriously. If their flags and banners move about erratically, they are on the verge of chaos. If their officers are short-tempered, they are succumbing to fatigue. If they feed the grain meant for human consumption to their horses and slaughter them for meat, if they don't bother to hang up their cooking utensils and do not return to their camp, they are in desperate straits. If the enemy's soldiers huddle together in small groups, whispering discreetly among themselves, their general has lost the confidence of his troops. If the enemy hands out rewards repeatedly, they are in difficulty. If they hand out punishments repeatedly, they are hard-pressed. If the officers first treat their troops cruelly but later are in fear of them, this is the height of incompetence. If the enemy's envoys act in a conciliatory manner, they want to end hostilities. If the enemy aggressively advances but continues neither to join battle nor retreat, this is something that must be carefully investigated and studied.

"In war, numerical superiority alone affords no clear advantage. If you avoid attacks that rely on military power alone, unify your forces, and properly assess the enemy, you will be able to take them. If you do not think things through

行軍

and take the enemy lightly, you surely will end up being captured.

"If you punish your troops before winning their affection, they will not submit to your authority.[9] If they do not submit to your authority, you will be unable to command them. If you win the affection of your troops but fail to administer appropriate punishments, you will not be able to command them. And so, lead them with civility and fairly apply martial discipline. This is known as 'the sure path to success.'

"If you instruct your subordinates with consistently administered orders, they will submit to your authority.[10] If you instruct your subordinates with inconsistently administered orders, they will not submit to your authority. A general whose orders are consistently administered will have excellent rapport with his troops."

Chapter 10

Dispositions of Terrain

Master Sun said,

"Among types of terrain there are: open, entangling, stalemated, constricted, dangerous, and distant.[1] Terrain upon which my forces as well as the enemy's can easily come and go is called 'open.' The disposition of open terrain is such that the first to take up positions within it that occupy the high ground, face south, and provide the best routes for supply will have the advantage in battle. Terrain that is easy to enter but difficult to return from is called 'entangling.' The disposition of entangling terrain is such that if the enemy is unprepared, I can attack and defeat them. If the enemy is prepared, and I attack without defeating them, it will be difficult for me to return from my attack, and I will be at a disadvantage. Terrain that offers neither me nor the enemy an advantage to enter is called 'stalemated.' The disposition of stalemated terrain is such that even if

地形

the enemy offers me some advantage, I will not
enter. Instead, I will try to lure them out by
marching off. Once half their troops have come
forth, I will have the advantage if I attack. The
disposition of 'constricted' terrain is such that
if I enter it first, I must occupy the entire area
with my troops. If the enemy enters first and
occupies the entire area I will not follow them
in. If they do not occupy the entire area, I will
follow them in. The disposition of 'dangerous'
terrain is such that if I occupy it first I must
take the high ground, facing south and wait
for the enemy. If the enemy occupies it first,
I will try to draw them out by marching off.
I will not follow them in. The disposition of
'distant' terrain is such that strategic potential[2]
is equally distributed; this makes it difficult to
join in battle. If you join in battle, there is no
advantage. These six describe ways to handle
terrain. It is a general's highest duty to investigate and study them!

"Among types of armies[3] there are: fleeing,
unstrung, sunken, collapsed, disorderly, and
routed. None of these six is the result of some
natural disaster; they all are brought about
through the failure of some general.

"When strategic potential is equally distributed, if one force attacks another ten times

its strength, the result will be what is called a 'fleeing' army. If the troops are strong but their leaders are weak, the result will be what is called an 'unstrung' army.[4] If the leaders are strong but the troops are weak, the result will be what is called a 'sunken' army. If the senior officers are angry with the general and insubordinate, when they encounter the enemy they will attack on their own without the general knowing their true capability. The result will be what is called a 'collapsed' army. If the general is weak and lacking in discipline, his instructions and guidance unclear, and he is inconsistent in the policies and orders he issues to both officers and troops, the ranks and formations will be confused and slovenly. The result will be what is called a 'disorderly' army. If a general proves incapable of properly assessing the enemy, dispatches a small force to engage a large and a weak force to engage a strong, and does not put his crack troops in the vanguard, the result will be what is called a 'routed' army. These six describe ways that lead to defeat. It is a general's highest duty to investigate and study them!

"The dispositions of terrain offer critical support to an army. Being able to assess the enemy in order to ensure victory and accounting for the danger, difficulty, and distance of terrain is the

地形

way of the superior general. Those who understand this and engage in battle are sure to be victorious. Those who fail to understand this and engage in battle are sure to be defeated.

"If you are certain you will be victorious in a battle but your ruler says not to fight, you should fight. If you are certain you cannot be victorious but your ruler says to fight, you should not fight. And so, a general who attacks without seeking to enhance his reputation and retreats without seeking to avoid blame, whose sole interest is the welfare of his troops and only aim is to benefit his ruler—such a general is a state treasure.

"Look upon your troops as your newborn babes and they will follow you into the deepest valleys; look upon your troops as your beloved children, and they will stand together with you unto death. If you are generous to them without putting them to work, if you love them but cannot command them, if you allow them to be disorderly and are unable to control them, they will be like spoiled children and utterly useless.

"If you know your troops are ready to attack but don't know the enemy is not vulnerable, you are only halfway to victory. If you know the enemy is vulnerable but don't know your troops are not ready to attack, you are only halfway to victory. If you know the enemy is vulnerable and your troops are ready to attack but don't know the disposition of the terrain is not conducive to battle, you are only halfway to victory.

"And so, those who understand military operations move but never lose their way, act but never run short of resources. This is why it is said, 'If you know the enemy and yourself, victory will never be in jeopardy. If you know the weather and the terrain,[5] victory will always be assured.'"

Chapter 11

Nine Types of Terrain

Master Sun said,

"Whenever you deploy your troops, [you may encounter]: dispersing terrain, easy terrain, contested terrain, accessible terrain, key terrain, serious terrain, difficult terrain, encircling terrain, and deadly terrain.[1]

"When the feudal lords fight upon their own territory, this is dispersing terrain.[2] When an army enters into enemy territory but not deeply, this is easy terrain.[3] When it is equally advantageous for me or for the enemy to take a piece of territory, this is contested terrain. When it is equally easy for me or for the enemy to enter or leave a piece of territory, this is accessible terrain. When the territory of a feudal lord borders three other states, so that the one who takes it can gain the entire empire, this is key terrain. When an army enters deeply into enemy territory, leaving far behind many of its

九
地

cities and towns, this is serious terrain. When an army marches across mountains, forests, cliffs, obstructions, marshes, or swamps, or any other course that is difficult to traverse, this is difficult terrain. When the only way into an area is a narrow pass and the only way out a circuitous route, where even a large force can be attacked by small enemy forces, this is encircling terrain. When fierce fighting means survival and anything less means death, this is deadly terrain.

"When on dispersing terrain, do not fight. When on easy terrain, do not halt. When on contested terrain, do not attack. When on accessible terrain, keep close intervals within your formations. When on key terrain, form alliances. When on serious terrain, plunder. When on difficult terrain, keep marching. When on encircling terrain, make plans. When on deadly terrain, fight!

"Those known as 'past masters of deploy-ing troops' were able to prevent their enemy's forward and rear units from uniting with one another, their large and small units from coor-dinating with one another, their officers and enlisted men from supporting one another, and their higher and lower echelons from cooperat-ing with one another. They caused their enemy's

forces to be fragmented and incapable of pulling themselves together, and ensured that those
few troops who did manage to pull themselves
together were unable to do so in an organized
and systematic manner. When it was to their
advantage, these past masters acted. When it
was not, they did not move."

May I ask,[4] "If a large, well-ordered enemy
force is about to attack, how should I prepare
to meet it?"

The response is, "First, seize something
they hold dear; then they will listen to your
demands."

"Speed is essential in war. Take advantage of
the enemy's lack of preparation, approach by
unexpected routes, and attack in places left
unguarded.

"When you are the invading force and have
penetrated deep into enemy territory, your
troops will be strongly united; the enemy
cannot defeat you. Plunder the riches of their
fields to ensure your army has adequate provisions. Nourish your troops and do not wear
them out. Conserve their energy and shepherd
their strength. Ensure that the movements
of your forces and the plans that you make
cannot be fathomed. Since you have placed

your troops in a position from which there is no way out, they will die before showing their backs to the enemy. When facing the threat of death, what soldier does not give his last ounce of strength? When troops are under the gravest threat, they are not afraid. When there is no way out, they stand firm. When they are deep in enemy territory, they bind together. When there is no choice, they fight!

"For this reason, such troops are vigilant without being trained, responsible without being held accountable, committed without prior agreement, and reliable without being under orders.[5] Prohibit fortune telling and cast out doubt and your troops will stand with you unto death. My officers are willing to give up great wealth, but not because they dislike property. They are willing to sacrifice long life, but not because they dislike longevity. On the day the order to march is issued, the tears of those who are seated drench their collars, while the tears of those who are reclining stream down to their chins, but place them in a position from which there is no way out and they all will display the courage of Zhuan Zhu and Cao Gui.[6]

"Those good at deploying troops take as their model the *Shuairan* 率然, a snake that lives on Mount Heng.[7] If you strike its head, the tail

will whip you. If you strike its tail, the head
will bite you. If you strike it in the middle,
both head and tail will attack."

May I ask, "Can an army be made to respond
as the *Shuairan* does?"

The response is, "Yes. The men of Wu and
Yue hate one another, but if they are crossing the sea in the same boat and encounter
dangerous headwinds, they will help each
other, just as the right hand helps the left."

"And so, tethering the horses together or bury-
ing the wheels of chariots[8] are not reliable
methods for maintaining one's ranks. To unite
the strength and courage of one's troops and
ensure that they act as one is the result of properly controlling them. To get the most out of
both the strongest and weakest of your troops
is the result of making proper use of terrain.

"And so, one who is good at deploying troops
gets them to join hands and work together as
one by leaving them no other choice but to do
so.

"The business of a general is to be calm and
inscrutable, correct and principled. He befud-
dles the ears and eyes of his officers and men
in order to keep them in the dark.[9] He changes

九
地

his affairs and alters his plans to keep people from knowing his intentions. He shifts the location of his camp and marches along a circuitous route so that people cannot lay plans. He prepares his men for battle as if they had climbed to a high place, and he had kicked away the ladder behind them. He leads them deep into the territory of the opposing feudal lords and releases the trigger.[10] He burns his ships and breaks his pots, driving his men forward as if they were a flock of sheep. He drives them this way and that, but none knows where he ultimately intends to go. He assembles the host of his army and places them in danger; this is the business of a general.

"The nine types of terrain, the relative advantages of deploying and maneuvering on them in different ways, and the principles of human emotions in response to them—these are things that must be carefully investigated and studied.

"When you are the invading force, if you penetrate deep into enemy territory, your troops will be strongly united; if your penetration is shallow, they will be more likely to disperse.[11]

"When you lead your forces out of your own state and cross into another's territory, this is cutoff terrain. When you can travel easily in any direction, this is key terrain. When you enter deeply into another's territory, this is serious terrain. When you enter but penetration is shallow, this is easy terrain. When there are strongly held positions to the rear and only narrow passes to the front, this is encircling terrain. When there is no way out, this is deadly terrain.

"And so, when on dispersing terrain, work to unify the commitment of your troops. When on easy terrain, ensure they stay in close contact. On contested ground, bring up the rear. On accessible terrain, keep them on guard. On key terrain, strengthen alliances. On serious terrain, make sure they have a secure supply of provisions. On difficult terrain, hurry them along. On encircling terrain, block any routes of escape the enemy may offer.[12] On deadly terrain, make clear the need to fight to the death.

"And so, the psychology of an army is such that when encircled, they resist; when they have no other choice, they fight; when deep in enemy territory, they obey.

"Those who do not know the plans of the feudal lords cannot form alliances with them.[13] Those

九
地

who do not know the disposition of mountains, forests, cliffs, obstructions, marshes, or swamps cannot maneuver an army. Those who do not avail themselves of local guides cannot gain the advantages of the terrain. Ignorance of any one of these three makes one unworthy to lead the army of a hegemonic lord.[14]

"When the army of a hegemonic lord attacks one of the great states, it prevents the enemy from assembling the bulk of its forces and so overawes them that they are incapable of forming alliances.

"And so, a hegemonic lord does not compete with the other states of the world in forming alliances and does not seek to increase his authority over the other states of the world. He trusts only in his own ambitions and overawes his enemies. As a result, he is able to take the cities and destroy the states of those who oppose him.

"Bestow rewards without concern about precedent and issue orders without paying attention to procedure. Use the host of the army as if it were a single man. Use them to accomplish things without telling them why. Use them to pursue advantage, without telling them of the dangers. Assign them to territory you have lost and they will survive. Commit them to deadly terrain and they will live. When an army is committed to a dangerous cause it can snatch victory from the jaws of defeat.

"The prime concern in war is carefully attending to the enemy's intentions. Focus your attack on a single point and from a distance of a thousand leagues strike and kill their general. This is known as 'using cleverness to achieve success.' On the day that war is declared, close the borders, destroy all passports, and cut off communication with your enemy's envoys. Retreat into the ancestral temple[15] and meticulously review every detail of your plan. If the enemy presents you with an opening, exploit it immediately. First, seize something they hold dear[16] and refuse to parley. Adjust your tactics in response to their movements and thereby determine the outcome of the battle.

"And so, in the early stages, be as coy as a maiden, but later, when the enemy opens the door, be as swift as a bolting rabbit. They will be incapable of opposing you."

Chapter 12

Attacking with Fire[1]

Master Sun said,

"There are five ways to attack using fire:[2] setting fire to personnel, setting fire to provisions, setting fire to supply wagons, setting fire to storehouses, and setting fire to concentrations of forces.[3] You must have a clear reason for attacking with fire, and you must prepare beforehand all the material and equipment needed for such an attack. There are right times and proper periods for using fire to attack. The right time is when the weather is hot and dry. The proper period is when the moon appears in the Winnowing Basket, Wall, Wings, or Chariot lunar lodge.[4] When the moon is in one of these lodges, the wind will pick up.

"Whenever you use fire to attack, you must respond appropriately to the various permutations of the five ways to attack. If you can set fire inside the enemy's camp or city, respond

火攻

quickly with an attack from outside. If the enemy's troops remain calm despite the fire, wait, and do not attack. Once the fire has peaked in strength, if conditions are right, follow up with an attack. If conditions are not right, hold your attack. You can set fire to enemy targets outside their camp or city without waiting to set fires inside. Set such fires whenever the time is right.[5] If you set fires upwind, do not attack downwind. If a wind has been blowing all day it will grow still at night. All armies must understand the various permutations of the five ways to attack using fire and employ them at the right times and proper periods.

"Using fire to support an attack brings clear and predictable results; using water to support an attack brings dramatic and powerful results. Water can carve up and cut off an enemy, but it cannot deprive them of their equipment and supplies.

"It is ominous to win a battle or take an objective but fail to follow through on such achievements. This is called 'wasteful procrastination.' And so it is said, 'An enlightened ruler reflects carefully; a great general follows through.'

"If it is not in the interest of the state, do not mobilize your army. If you cannot take your objective, do not deploy your troops. If the state is not threatened, do not go to war. A ruler should not raise an army out of anger; a general should not fight a battle out of resentment.[6] If it is in the interest of the state, mobilize your army; if it is not in the interest of the state, take no action. Those who are angry can again be happy. Those who seethe with resentment can again feel joy. A lost state, though, cannot be brought back into existence and the dead cannot be brought back to life. And so, an enlightened ruler is careful about feelings of anger and a great general is cautious about harboring resentment. This is the way to keep the state at peace and the army intact."

Chapter 13

On the Use of Spies

Master Sun said,

"When you raise an army of a hundred thousand men and send them off on a distant campaign a thousand leagues away, the cost to private households and public coffers will come to a thousand pieces of gold a day. There will be great turmoil throughout the state, people will wear themselves out transporting supplies on the highways and roads, and some seven hundred thousand households will be unable to attend to their normal affairs.[1] Opposing forces can battle each other for years in order to win victory decided upon a single day. And yet some, who covet high office and salary or begrudge but a hundred pieces of gold, will fail to use spies to ascertain the enemy's situation and condition.[2] This is the height of inhumanity! Such people are not fit to serve as generals; they are not true counselors, nor are they masters of victory.

用
間

"What enables the enlightened ruler or worthy general to conquer others whenever they deploy their forces and realize achievements that far surpass the common run of men is that they know things beforehand. Such knowledge cannot be obtained from ghosts or spirits, it is not prefigured in situations or events nor can one determine it through calculation—it must be gained from people who know the enemy's situation and condition.

"And so, there are five types of spies that one can use: local, inside, double, dead, and live. If all five types of spies are working at the same time and no one knows of their activities, this is called 'a divine net' and is a ruler's treasure.[3]

"Local spies are agents you recruit from among the local population. Inside spies are officials you recruit from within the enemy's own ranks. Double agents are enemy spies you successfully recruit to your side. Dead spies are your own agents who are provided with false information to be given to the enemy.[4] Live spies are agents who can return and report to you about the enemy's situation and condition.

"And so, within the army, no one is closer to the ruler than his spies, no one is rewarded more lavishly, and no one is more secretive. If one is not sagely and wise, one cannot use spies. If one is not benevolent and righteous, one cannot deploy spies. If one is not subtle and sensitive, one cannot get the truth out of spies. How subtle! How subtle! Spies can be used everywhere! If confidential information about a spy's mission is prematurely disclosed, the spy and all those told about the mission must be put to death.

"Whenever there is an army you want to attack, a city you want to lay siege to, or a person you want to assassinate, you first must know the family and personal names of your enemy's commanding general, his closest associates, messengers, gatekeepers, and attendants. Dispatch your spies to search out and discover as much as you can about them. You also must discover those the enemy has sent to spy on you. You must attract them with bribes and persuade them to defect to your side. In this way, you can gain double agents and put them to use. By employing such double agents to further understand the enemy, you can gain local and inside spies and make use of them. By employing local and inside spies to further understand the enemy, you can find ways for your dead spies to convey false information to them. By employing your dead

用
間

spies to further understand the enemy, your live spies can tell you of your enemy's plans when they return at the appointed time.

"A ruler must be well-informed about the work of the five types of spies, and the key to his being well-informed is the double agent. And so, double agents must be rewarded the most lavishly of all.

"In the past, the Yin flourished because it made use of Yi Zhi, who was serving the Xia; the Zhou flourished because it made use of Lü Ya, who was serving the Yin.[5] And so, only the enlightened ruler and worthy general, who are capable of getting the most wise to serve as their spies, always succeed in producing great achievements. This is essential in war and what an army relies upon in order to take action."

Notes

Chapter 1

1. In the traditional version of the text, there is only one character in the title of this chapter, as here. The later *Military Classics* edition adds the character *shi* 始 thus giving as the title: "Initial Assessments" (*shi ji* 始計).

2. The word translated "and so" is *gu* 故. While *gu* and related terms such as *shi yi* 是以 often function to introduce implications of what has come before, they less often indicate the start of a genuine conclusion. And so, while commonly translated "therefore," in most cases, this is too strong and misleading. D. C. Lau has pointed out that in composite texts, like *Master Sun's Art of War, gu* and its relatives often serve as a kind of textual glue used by editors to tie together disparate material. When these terms function in this way, I have simply not translated them. For Lau's insights regarding *gu* and related terms, see D. C. Lau, trans., *Lao Tzu: Tao Te Ching*, Reprint (London: Penguin Books, 1974), 172–73.

3. The word translated "weather" (*tian* 天) can also be understood as heaven. In this context, though, it clearly means atmospheric conditions.

4. Here and in numerous places throughout the text, Sunzi recognizes and values ethical aspects of war, especially, though not exclusively, in regard to leadership. This is important to keep in mind as he often is depicted as a cool and calculating amoralist, interested only in strategy and victory.

5. *Yin* 陰 and *yang* 陽 are the two elemental forces. Among *yin*'s characteristics are being dark, still, hidden, and feminine; among *yang*'s characteristics are being bright, active, clear, and masculine.

6. How to deploy and maneuver one's troops on different kinds of terrain is a central theme of later chapters. See especially Chapters 9 through 11.

7. These passages make clear that people like Sunzi served as roving military counselors or consultants who sought employment in the courts of different rulers.

Notes

8. "Strategic potential" (*shi* 勢) refers to the inherent power that is latent in certain situations or conditions. At times, it can refer more to the situations or conditions themselves, but the idea of the hidden power within such situations or conditions is key to understanding the concept. See the discussion in the Introduction and Chapter 5.

9. The ancestral temple is where ancestral tablets were kept and where important sacrifices to the ancestors took place. It is also where the most important affairs of state were decided. Here, Sunzi is concerned with the final strategic calculations before going to war. He is not endorsing or advocating any type of divination, a practice which he thinks has no place in war.

Chapter 2

1. "Leagues" is the translation for *li* 里, a unit of length equal to about half a kilometer.

2. They never have to make such additional appeals because they have laid careful plans that ensure a swift and decisive victory and avoid protracted campaigns.

3. This is one of several anonymous common sayings that are cited in the text.

Chapter 4

1. In autumn, animals grow their winter pelts, which have the finest and hence the lightest hair.

2. Because they did not engage an enemy unless they knew they could win and laid the groundwork needed to ensure victory.

3. The ratio implied is more like a pound to ten grains, but we are interested in the sense and not the precise weights.

Chapter 5

1. Regular (*zheng* 正) and special (*qi* 奇) forces refer both to types of units as well as their functions. Regular forces or operations engage and occupy the enemy, setting him up for decisive blows delivered by special forces. These two terms appear with related senses in other works of this period. For example, compare the opening lines of chapter 57 of the *Daodejing*: "Follow what is correct and regular (*zheng*) in ordering your state. Follow what is strange and perverse (*qi*) in deploying your troops" or the following line from chapter 58, "What is correct and regular (*zheng*) turns strange and perverse (*qi*)."

2. For these terms of art, see the "Prominent Ideas" section of the Introduction. The pair of terms serves as the title and theme of the next chapter.

3. Early Chinese music employed a pentatonic scale whose notes are called *gong* 宮, *shang* 商, *jue* 角, *zhi* 徵, and *yu* 羽.

4. The traditional list of colors is black, red, blue-green, white, and yellow.

5. The traditional list of tastes is bitter, sour, salty, sweet, and spicy.

6. The idea is that these two types of forces are the fundamental elements and basic constituents of any battle.

7. The force of pent-up water that is suddenly released possesses tremendous power and momentum. Here we see the point, discussed in the Introduction, about how strategic potential always points to or implies the inherent power in a condition or situation.

Chapter 6

1. On the terms in this chapter title, see note 2 of Chapter 5. While the terms themselves do not appear often, much of the chapter concerns how these ideas function in war. One is to remain "tenuous" in the eyes of one's enemy, to the point where one's troops and intentions seem to vanish into thin air. And yet, one must be prepared to gather one's troops and one's resolve together swiftly and decisively to create a mighty and solid force that can crush one's enemy.

One should attack the enemy where his force is most tenuous: in his "soft spots," while remaining solid and impregnable in defense.

2. The word translated "form" here (*xing* 形) is the same word translated "disposition of forces" elsewhere. Compare to note 5 below. The idea is that the disposition of one's forces is the "form" or "shape" of one's forces.

3. This is a good illustration of "solidity" and "tenuousness." An enemy secure in a fortress represents "solidity" to avoid. Attack a "tenuous" or soft spot, which the enemy must then relieve with reinforcements, opening an advantage to exploit.

4. Yue was the large southernmost state in ancient China. The region "south of Yue" (*Yue nan* 越南, in the Vietnamese language, *Viet nam*), became the state of Vietnam.

5. Here "shape or form" is the English rendering of the word translated "disposition of forces" earlier in the sentence and throughout the text. Compare note 2.

6. Here we see reference to the notions of both strategic potential (*shi* 勢) and disposition of forces (*xing* 形). In this context, the latter refers to states of water, and so I have translated it "disposition or form."

7. They are "spirit-like" (*shen* 神) in that they are able to accomplish their aims without any discernable action. Compare the earlier passage in this chapter that describes superior warriors, who are "so spirit-like."

8. The five phases are fundamental forces in traditional Chinese metaphysics. They pass through a series in which one "overcomes" another. The five are metal, wood, water, fire, and earth. Metal overcomes wood, wood overcomes earth, earth overcomes water, water overcomes fire, fire overcomes metal. The point here is that no one of the five dominates all the others.

Chapter 7

1. The idea is that rushing one's forces into a battle tempted by the potential of some limited gain puts you at a severe disadvantage. The next line describes a similar case of being lured into an impetuous and foolish attack.

2. On a forced march, troops carry a minimum of supplies and leave their heavy armor at their base camp to move swiftly over long distances.

3. In each of these three scenarios, the point is that forced marches leave you with only a fraction of your total force on hand and ready to engage the enemy. Thus, such strategies often fail and are always risky.

4. *Yin* is one of the two elemental forces *yin* 陰 and *yang* 陽. See Chapter I, note 5.

5. The reference is to some lost military text.

6. "Heart and mind" is the translation of the Chinese word *xin* 心, which traditionally was thought to contain affective, cognitive, and volitional faculties. Compare *Analects* 9.26: "You can take a general away from his army, but you cannot take a firm resolve away from an ordinary man." The notion of having one's heart and mind taken away is revisited in the next section.

7. The original says, "Always leave a surrounded enemy a way out." I have changed it to the prohibitive form out of stylistic concerns. The meaning is unchanged.

Chapter 8

I. The opening lines of this chapter are identical to those that open Chapter 7.

2. Deadly terrain refers to ground which leaves no way out, where the only alternatives are victory or death. Compare the opening sections of Chapter II.

3. Commentators are divided over what these nine are. The most reasonable reference would seem to be found in the nine recommendations above about how to handle different types of terrain (i.e., the previous ten lines less the last, about orders). The reader is encouraged to compare Chapter II, which is devoted to this issue.

4. On this issue, too, commentators differ in their explanations. One possibility

is the advantages regarding roads, armies, cities, types of ground, and orders listed above.

Chapter 9

1. This will offer your troops a bit more warmth.

2. So they cannot be pinned against the water.

3. This way, you face only half their number and the remaining half are mired in the water. Compare the example, discussed in the Introduction, of the Duke of Song, who insisted that one must allow one's foe to ford and assemble their ranks before attacking.

4. So that you can be sure to have adequate supplies of water, fodder, kindling, and lumber.

5. Infantrymen carrying shields on their left can protect themselves as they retreat toward the right or back.

6. The Yellow Emperor is a legendary culture hero and ideal sovereign. Said to have lived from 2697 to 2597 BCE, he is claimed as the progenitor of the Han Chinese race. Among his many purported inventions are armor and weapons. He fought famous battles against the malevolent forces of Yandi and Chi You. The final phrase "in all the four directions" is an interpretation of two characters that literally mean "Four Emperors" (*si di* 四帝). Because there is no clear reference for these two characters, I understand them as saying the four ways of deploying troops enabled the Yellow Emperor to defeat the rulers who opposed him on all four sides, i.e., throughout the realm.

7. Aside from the first and last, we cannot be certain what these six terrain features refer to, but it is likely that the remaining four are something like sinkholes, box canyons, areas of dense vegetation, and unstable regions that might collapse when traveled over.

8. Because the enemy is cutting down trees along the way to clear the road or to use as lumber.

9. This section presents Sunzi's views about the need for brotherhood and camaraderie among troops and officers. This aspect of his thought is more

Confucian in character but often goes unnoticed because of later caricatures of Sunzi as a cool and ruthless strategist.

10. Compare what Sunzi says here and in the previous section with the following passage from chapter 10 of the *Xunzi*: "And so, if you punish without first instructing, your punishments will grow numerous, but you will not conquer depravity. If you instruct without proper punishment, criminals will not be deterred."

Chapter 10

1. Commentators disagree about what each of these types of terrain describe. Their various views are highly speculative, and so I leave it to the reader to imagine what Sunzi may have in mind in each case.

2. For the notion of "strategic potential," see Chapter 5.

3. As is clear, these are types of defeated or demoralized armies.

4. "Unstrung" is a literal translation of *chi* 弛 and offers a striking metaphor, for an army without strong leaders is like a powerful bow that has not been readied to shoot.

5. As earlier, "weather" is literally "heaven" (*tian* 天) and here is contrasted with "terrain," literally "earth" (*di* 地). And so, the last line also has the sense "If you understand heaven and earth, victory will always be assured."

Chapter 11

1. As will become clear from the following descriptions, the focus here is on the effects different types of terrain have on the psychology of troops. In this respect, this chapter's discussion of types of terrain differs from the previous in which the focus was more the features of the terrain itself. For "deadly terrain," compare the opening section of Chapter 8.

2. This type of terrain is so named because troops are tempted to disperse by returning to their homes which are nearby.

Notes

3. This type of terrain is so named because the troops are not far from home and so still at ease.

4. This question and answer format is seen in a couple of passages in the text and is another clue pointing to its composite nature.

5. Such troops spontaneously do what a general wants because their fates are bound together and the general demonstrates sincere concern for them.

6. Zhuan Zhu 專諸 was a famous warrior from the Spring and Autumn Period. He was from the state of Wu and renowned for his courage. Cao Gui 曹劌, also known as Cao Mo 曹沫, was a famous warrior from the same time and with a similar reputation, from the state of Lu. Their biographies appear in chapter 86 of Sima Qian's 司馬遷 *The Grand Scribe's Records* (*Shiji* 史記). For English translations, see William H. Nienhauser, Jr., ed., *The Grand Scribe's Records*, Vol. 7 (Bloomington: Indiana University Press, 1994): 319–21.

7. The text has *chang* 常 in place of *heng* 恆 because of the taboo against mentioning the Western Han Dynasty emperor Wen Di's (r. 179–157 BCE) personal name (Liu Heng 劉恆). Mount Heng is the northernmost of the five sacred peaks and is located in Shanxi province.

8. These are methods designed to express the resolve of troops to stand and fight.

9. The idea that a ruler should keep his subjects in the dark and without knowledge is a theme in the *Daodejing* (see, for example, chapters 3 and 65). In the *Daodejing*, being without knowledge is offered as an ideal and characteristic of the sage as well (e.g., chapter 20). The thought is that natural actions are not based on knowledge and deliberation but spontaneously flow as responses to whatever arises. Han Fei Zi 韓非子 (ca. 280–233 BCE) advocated a similar practice but for very different reasons. He thought a ruler must conceal his plans not only from his enemies and subordinates, but even from his intimates as well to keep them from exploiting such knowledge to his disadvantage and to preserve his persona as all-powerful and mysterious lord. For a study that explores these aspects of his philosophy, see my "Hanfeizi and Moral Self-Cultivation" in *Lehalist Philosophy of Han Fei, Journal of Chinese Philosophy*, 38.1 (March 2011): 49–63. Sunzi seems to be motivated in part by these kinds of ideas but also from a more general concern with operational security and the threat of espionage—concerns which are made explicit in Chapter 13.

10. The idea is that the general gives his men the impression that they cannot turn back; like an arrow released from a crossbow, they are to fly forward into battle.

11. This section and the next show some considerable overlap with the opening sections of the chapter; parts seem corrupt and these sections appear to be out of place.

12. An encircling army traditionally offers exit routes for troops that want to surrender and leave the field of battle. Sunzi advises generals to block these to show that there is only one way out: by fighting.

13. The lines in this section appear as part of Chapter 7.

14. Reading 此三者 for 四五者. A "hegemonic lord" was the ruler of a state who could unify the other states around him and rule as de facto emperor, but without having to depose and overthrow the powerless Zhou king.

15. See the concluding section of Chapter 1.

16. The same idea appears earlier in this chapter.

Chapter 12

1. As noted in the Introduction, this is the only chapter dedicated to a particular type of weapon, as opposed to general issues of organization, politics, and strategy.

2. The most celebrated example in Chinese history of the use of fire as a weapon is the battle of Red Cliffs. The most complete historical account of this engagement is found in the *Records of the Three Kingdoms* (*Sanguo zhi* 三國志) and an embellished and widely read account is found in the *Romance of the Three Kingdoms* (*Sanguo yanyi* 三國演義). The battle was fought at the end of the Han Dynasty, around 208 CE, between the allied forces of Liu Bei and Sun Quan on one side and Cao Cao on the other, Cao Cao being the author of the earliest commentary on *Master Sun's Art of War*. Cao Cao was decisively defeated when his moored ships were burned by way of a clever strategy employed by Liu Bei and Sun Quan. For a modern analysis of Cao Cao as a strategist, which includes

a discussion of this action, see Karl W. Eikenberry, "The Campaigns of Cao Cao," *Military Review* 74, no. 8 (1994): 56–64.

3. That is, on troops on the march, encamped, or in reserve.

4. The lunar lodge system divided the sky into twenty-eight sectors. The system is roughly equivalent to the twelve constellations of the Western zodiac, except that it defined the path of the moon in the lunar calendar rather than the sun in the solar.

5. A reference to the "right times and proper periods" described above.

6. Sunzi tells us that the great general is to avoid feelings of resentment (*yun* 慍), a sense that one's abilities are unacknowledged or underappreciated. Compare the last line of the opening passage of the *Analects*, which says: "One whose talents are unacknowledged and yet harbors no resentment—is he not a gentleman?" The point is, a general should not fight with the aim of making a name for himself.

Chapter 13

1. Among the vital work that will be disrupted are things such as agriculture and weaving.

2. The thought is that such people would rather not risk their own position or salary or spend even a relatively small amount of money to secure the services of spies.

3. "Divine net" translates *shen ji* 神紀. Using all five types of spies is a "net" in that it allows the ruler to *draw in* information as a fisherman draws in fish with his net. It is "divine" in accomplishing its work in ways that do not rely on any discernable action. Compare note 7 of Chapter 6.

4. I take "dead" *si* 死 to indicate that one no longer has contact with these spies: one sends them off with misinformation but does not expect them to report back. In this way, they differ from "live" spies, the last type described. Commentators tend to take *si* as meaning these spies are most at risk and will almost certainly be killed.

5. The Yin refers to the Yin 殷 or Shang 商 Dynasties (1766–1122 BCE). The Xia refers to the Xia 夏 Dynasty (2205–1766 BCE) and the Zhou refers to the Zhou 周 Dynasty (1122–256 BCE). Yi Zhi 伊摯 (better known as Yi Yin 伊尹) was a minister of the Xia who defected to the Yin. Lü Ya 呂牙 or Lü Shang 呂尚 (better known as Jiang Ziya 姜子牙, Tai Gongwang 太公望, or Shi Shangfu 師尚父) was a minister of the Yin who crossed over to the Zhou. Normally, loyalty would require a minister to die with his lord, much less spy for the enemy, but these two men are generally regarded as exceptions because they recognized that the rulers they first served were fundamentally corrupt. For Yi Zhi, see *Mengzi* 5A6, etc. Lü Ya's biography appears in chapter 32 of Sima Qian's *The Grand Scribe's Records* (*Shiji* 史記). For an English translation, see William H. Nienhauser, Jr., ed., *The Grand Scribe's Records*, Volume V. I (Bloomington: Indiana University Press, 2006): 31–130.

Recommended Readings

General Background

Graham, Angus C. *Disputers of the Tao: Philosophical Argument in Ancient China*. La Salle, IL: Open Court, 1989.

Loewe, Michael, and Edward L. Shaughnessy, eds. *The Cambridge History of Ancient China: From the Origins of Civilization to 221 B.C.* Cambridge: Cambridge University Press, 1999.

Olberding, Amy L., and Philip J. Ivanhoe, eds. *Mortality and Traditional China*. Albany: State University of New York Press, 2011.

Schwartz, Benjamin I. *The World of Thought in Ancient China*. Cambridge, MA: Belknap Press, 1985.

Works on War in Traditional China

Bell, Daniel A. "Just War and Confucianism: Implications for the Contemporary World." In *Beyond Liberal Democracy: Political Thinking for an East Asian Context*, 23–51. Princeton, NJ: Princeton University Press, 2006.

Di Cosmo, Nicola, ed. *Military Culture in Imperial China*. Cambridge, MA: Harvard University Press, 2009.

Eikenberry, Karl W. "The Campaigns of Cao Cao." *Military Review* 74, no. 8 (1994): 56–64.

Hong, Yang. *Weapons in Ancient China*. New York: Beijing Science Press, 1992.

Kierman, Frank A., and John K. Fairbank, eds. *Chinese Ways in Warfare*. Cambridge, MA: Harvard University Press, 1974.

Lau, D. C., and Roger T. Ames. *Sun Bin: The Art of Warfare: A Translation of the Classic Chinese Work of Philosophy and Strategy*. New York: Ballantine Books, 1996.

Lewis, Mark Edward. *Sanctioned Violence in Early China*. Albany: State University of New York Press, 1990.

Petersen, Jens Østergaard. "What's in a Name?: On the Sources Concerning Sun Wu." *Asia Major*, Third Series, 5, no. I (1992): I–31.

Rand, Christopher C. "Chinese Military Thought and Philosophical Taoism." *Monumenta Serica* 34 (1979–80): 171–218.

Sawyer, Ralph D. *The Seven Military Classics of Ancient China*. Boulder, CO: Westview Press, 1993.

Yu, Kam-por. "Confucian Views on War as Seen in the *Gongyang Commentary on the Spring and Autumn Annals*." *DAO: A Journal of Comparative Philosophy* 9, no. I (2010): 97–III.

Translations of *Master Sun's Art of War*

Ames, Roger T. *The Art of Warfare*. New York: Ballantine Books, 1993.

A highly readable translation with lengthy preface based upon recently excavated versions of the text.

Griffith, Samuel B., trans. *Sun Tzu: The Art of War*. Reprint. New York: Oxford University Press, 1971.

This translation includes many passages from traditional commentaries and provides very insightful introductions and appendixes on the text, its time, and later influences. The translator was a retired brigadier general in the U.S. Marine Corps and brought his sense and experience of war to the work, with excellent effect.

Mair, Victor, trans. *The Art of War: Sunzi's Military Methods*. New York: Columbia University Press, 2007.

This is the most thorough, scholarly treatment of the text, with a rich and lengthy introduction locating it within its historical context and within the larger frame of world literature on war.

Recommended Readings

Minford, John, trans. *The Art of War.* London: Penguin Books, 2003.

The most poetic translation, which succeeds in preserving much of the terseness the original often has. It includes a helpful introduction and reading aids and a second section which provides commentary on the text drawn not only from traditional commentaries but also contemporaneous texts.

Index

Index

Index

PHILIP J. IVANHOE is Professor of Philosophy in the Department of Public and Social Administration, City University of Hong Kong. He specializes in the history of East Asian philosophy and religion and its potential for contemporary ethics. He has written, edited, or co-edited more than twenty books and published more than fifty articles as well as numerous dictionary and encyclopedia entries on Chinese and Western religious and ethical thought. Among his publications are:

The Sense of Antirationalism: The Religious Thought of Zhuangzi and Kierkegaard, with Karen L. Carr, Createspace, 2010.

The Essays and Letters of Zhang Xuecheng (1738–1801), Stanford University Press, 2009.

Readings from the Lu-Wang School of Neo-Confucianism, Hackett Publishing Company, 2009. (Translations, with Introduction and notes).

Religious and Philosophical Aspects of the Laozi, with Mark Csikszentmihalyi, SUNY Press, 2009.

Confucian Moral Self Cultivation, 2nd edition, Hackett Publishing Company, 2006.

Ethics in the Confucian Tradition: The Thought of Mengzi and Wang Yangming, Hackett Publishing Company, 2002.

Laozi, *Daodejing,* Hackett Publishing Company, 2003. (Translation, with Introduction and notes).

Readings in Classical Chinese Philosophy, 2nd edition, with Bryan Van Norden, Hackett Publishing Company, 2006. (Anthology, with Introduction and notes).